"Hilarious, caring and compass~~~~
What more could you want from an acting coach?"
—BROC WIGINTON, *EVERYBODY HATES CHRIS*, AT&T, *HASBRO*

"I have a career in Hollywood because of Chambers. If I wouldn't have met him, it would never have happened. He helped me start it all."
—ALLISON SCAGLIOTTI SMITH, MINDY ON NICK'S *DRAKE AND JOSH*

"Working with Chambers is always a blast because he's so funny and you know he really cares about you He helped me be the best actor I can be."
—JOSH REEVES, *DESPERATE HOUSEWIVES*, *COLD CASE*

"Sure! Chambers is the most creative and innovative coach around. His energy and talent are amazing!"
—HAYLEY HOLMES, *ICARLY*, *HANNA MONTANA*, *TRAPPED IN TV GUIDE*

"Chambers is the Best of the Best! No matter who you are or where you come from, if you want it, he can help you. His coaching gets me the callback. Chambers will pull the star out of you, so get ready to shine."
—DEVANTE WARREN, *ZOEY 101*, *CURB YOUR ENTHUSIASM*

"Chambers and his books have really helped me progress in the short time I've been in Hollywood. He is truly a great acting coach and, not to mention, a great friend. His books are filled front to back with awesome scenes and info. I definitely recommend them all."
—MICHAEL MCSHAE, *HANNA MONTANA*, *MEDIUM*, *12 MILES OF BAD ROAD*

"Chambers is the Master of Comedy. Starring in my own TV series, I use his techniques daily."
—ALYX GAUDIO, STAR OF THE TV SERIES *JUSTIN TIME*

"Chambers has taught me a lot about how to focus, have energy and be creative. He not only inspires me to go out on a limb; he demands it."
—HANNAH MARKS, *UGLY BETTY*, *PRIVATE PRACTICE*, *CSI: MIAMI*

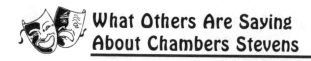

What Others Are Saying About Chambers Stevens

"Chambers Stevens is one of the most talented men I have ever known. His heart is as big as his talent. To work with him is a true joy. I wish everyone could have that experience."
—DAVID VAN HOOSER, MULTI EMMY AWARD-WINNING WRITER/DIRECTOR, GEORGE PEABODY AWARD WINNER

"Anyone who listens to Chambers Stevens walks away smarter, sharper and smiling. He can convey gobs of information all under the guise of 'having fun'. He never talks down to kids, and as a result, they all adore working for him. In my book that makes him the consummate kid teaching pro."
—SUSAN ANDERS, VOICE COACH, AUTHOR OF "SINGING WITH STYLE"

"He has an incredible knack for capturing the essence of being a kid or teen in his monologues. Whether comedy or drama, my kids find Chambers' writing relatable, timely, and fun. We have had great success using Chambers' monologues for agencies and casting directors in Los Angeles."
—SHARI HEINKE, MOM OF ACTORS SARAH HEINKE (THE VOICE OF STRAWBERRY SHORTCAKE) AND RYAN HEINKE (NORTH AVE ALLSTARS)

"I call Chambers "The Great Motivator" because above all else, I think his greatest gift is to have people believe in their own possibilities. His spirit, enthusiasm, and genuine interest in others infuses everyone he's around with the sense that they can be more than they are today. The great bonus is, with his coaching, they actually can."
—GREGORY BOULTON, OWNER OF THE BOULTON AGENCY

"Chambers continues to amaze me with his fantastic material. I'm particularly excited for this book, because in just a year, my daughter will be able to read it herself! Look out, world!"
—JULIAN PETRILLO, 1ST. ASST. DIRECTOR ON NICK'S UNFABULOUS

Hollywood 101

MAGNIFICENT MONOLOGUES for kids 2

"MORE Kids' Monologues For Every Occasion!"

by

Chambers Stevens

SANDCASTLE
PUBLISHING &
DISTRIBUTION
south pasadena, california

Magnificent Monologues for Kids 2 : More Kids' Monologues for Every Occasion!

Copyright © 2009 by Chambers Stevens

Book Cover & Interior Design by Renée Rolle-Whatley

Book Cover Photography by Nathan Hope

The images used herein were obtained from IMSI's Master Clips©/MasterPhotos© Collection, 1895 Francisco Blvd. East, San Rafael, CA 94901-5506, USA

Actors in Cover Photograph: Left-to-Right: <u>Back Row:</u> Ashley Walton, Kaitlin Jones, Stephan Markarian, Timmothy Mann, Sarah Goggans, Jameson Rossi; <u>Middle Row:</u> Jasmine Black, Dylan Whitehead, Juliann Lamb; <u>Front Row Seated:</u> Kurt Doss, Tristen Lankford

Published by: Sandcastle Publishing & Distribution

Post Office Box 3070

South Pasadena, CA 91031-6070

Phone/Website (323) 255-3616, www.ChildrenActingBooks.com

Publisher's Cataloging in Publication
(Provided by Quality Books, Inc.)

Stevens, Chambers.
      Magnificent monologues for kids. 2, More kids
monologues for every occasion / by Chambers Stevens. -- 1st ed.
      p. cm. -- (Hollywood 101)
      Includes bibliographical references and index.
      SUMMARY: A collection of short original monologues,
ranging from thirty seconds to two minutes in length,
intended for use by elementary school boys and girls in
the theatre arts.
      Audience: Ages 5-12.
      ISBN-13: 978-1-883995-14-0
      ISBN-10: 1-883995-14-0

      1. Monologues--Juvenile literature. 2. Acting--
Juvenile literature. [1. Monologues. 2. Acting.]
I. Title. II. Title: More kids monologues for every
occasion

PN2080.S742 2007   812'.608
                       QBI078-600084

First Printing 11/2008

Printed and bound in China
13 12 11 10 09 08   10 9 8 7 6 5 4 3 2 1

Table of Contents

Dedication

MARCELLA

"YOU HAVE TAUGHT MY WIFE, SON, AND I
THE TRUE MEANING OF FRIENDSHIP."

Congratulations! Since you are reading my forward that would mean you are wisely holding a copy of one of Chambers Stevens' incredible books. This means you are taking the pursuit of your career seriously and I applaud you for your efforts. As a director of film, television, and theater, my livelihood and passion center on the ability to work with wonderful actors. Many people say they want to be actors, but it is only a select few who study their craft and endeavor daily to achieve what, at times, might feel like the unachievable.

There are few acting coaches that I have ever come across that understand the business from the inside out as Chambers does. It never surprises me in an audition when the actors that impress me the most and stand out amongst their peers all have been students of Chambers Stevens. Chambers consistently sets the standards for other acting coaches and time and time again helps to raise the bar within the entertainment industry.

There are plenty of acting coaches out there and

plenty of books written to help guide an actor in his craft, but there truly is only one Chambers Stevens.

So do yourself a favor if you believe in yourself and your desire is to achieve longevity as an actor.

Buy this book.

And if you've already bought it, then what are you doing hanging out reading my forward? Skip a few pages and get crackin' with Chambers' work. And hopefully one day in an audition, you'll let me know personally that you liked what Chambers had to say.

— ANDY FICKMAN
AWARD-WINNING DIRECTOR, DISNEY'S
THE GAME PLAN, RACE TO WITCH MOUNTAIN **AND**
DREAMWORKS' *SHE'S THE MAN*

Introduction

Welcome to Hollywood 101's Magnificent Monologues for Kids 2.

It's been a few years since I wrote the first book in the Hollywood 101 series. And now you are holding my seventh book.

Since that first book, I have received thousands of emails from young actors thanking me for the books. Using my scenes, monologues, and commercials, many young actors have booked professional work (film, television, and theatre roles). Some have gotten parts in their school plays and some have even won awards.

Most of the emails I've received have asked me to write more. Well here they are: Magnificent Monologues For Kids 2. But this time I have added something extra. I've noticed that some auditions ask for a thirty-second monologue. Many of the monologues in my other books are longer than that. So this time I've included ten thirty-second monologues in case you need something shorter. And just like the other books, all of the monologues have been tested using professional young actors.

A lot has happened to me since I wrote my first book. I've been invited all over the United States and asked to do acting workshops. (If you or your theatre would like me to visit, please check out www.ChildrenActingBooks.com to find out more information). During these workshops, I have had the opportunity to see lots of monologues performed. How many, you say? 20,000! Yes, that's right, in the last eight years I have seen over 20,000 monologues performed. Some of them have been so fantastic, that I've stood up and given them a standing ovation. Others have been down right terrible. (I once saw an actor stop and start his monologue five times in thirty seconds!) Watching all of these monologues has helped me fine tune what works during an audition. And what

doesn't. So before you pick a monologue, make sure you read the "Helpful Hints For A Great Audition" section on page 6.

Now, one last thing. Many of you have written me emails asking about my life. How I got started as an actor. What kind of acting I did as a kid. And how I got to Hollywood.

Many people assume that because I now live in Hollywood, I must have been born in California. And that my parents must have worked in the show business industry.

The truth is far from that.

Like many of you, I am from a small town. My town is outside Nashville, Tennessee. My dad was a salesman and my mother was an artist that worked at home. Ever since I can remember, I wanted to be an actor. My parents were great, but they didn't know of any way to help me.

So for the first seven years of my life, I put on plays at home. I would use my stuffed animals, and I would create wild, silly plays about their lives. When my cousins came over, I forced them to watch my performances.

Then in second grade, I got my big break. I got the lead in the school play. But three days before I was to go on, I got chickenpox. So the teacher banned me from school and put my understudy in my place. I drove my mother crazy begging her to take me back to school. Finally, on the day of the performance I stole her makeup and covered up my pox and walked to school. The teacher thought I was cured and let me go on. I was a huge hit. Until everyone in my class got chickenpox.

I didn't get a chance to be in another play for seven more years. Seven years! But I didn't get depressed. I just continued putting on my own productions in my backyard. But now instead of stuffed animals, I used the kids around the neighborhood. When they got tired, I put on solo shows. And I would also read every book I could on acting. I read all of the plays in my school and my hometown library. When I read the last one, I begged the librarian to order some more. After a month she did, just to get me to stop driving her crazy.

In eighth grade, I got a role in another school play. But after all of the hard work I had done on my own for the last seven years, I did not get the lead. I got a small part! At first I was down, but then I remembered the phrase, "There are no small parts, just small actors." And I didn't want to be that. So I worked on my small part as hard as I could. And since I had so much free time, I helped build the sets and the costumes, hung curtains, and painted the floor. My hard work did not go unnoticed. On the next play, the director gave me the lead.

After a couple more plays, my parents took me to the big city of Nashville to find a real acting teacher. I was lucky to find a studio called THE ACTING STUDIO run by Ruth Sweet. Ruth was very tough. But it was good for me. She taught me discipline. And showed me how to audition and how to build a character. Most importantly, she showed me how to audition for a good college.

Now my dad did not want me to go to college to be an actor. He was hoping I would be a lawyer or…heck he wanted me to be ANYTHING but an actor. But he also loved me, so he made a bet with me.

He said he would pay for me to go to college under two conditions:

one, I would only audition for the best schools in the country; and two, if I didn't get in, I would go to law school. I nervously shook his hand and the bet was sealed.

Long story short, I got into all five of the schools I auditioned for. My dad was stuck, and he kept his end of the deal.

I picked the Conservatory of Theatre Arts at Webster University, which is near St. Louis. It was a great choice for me. Thanks to great teachers like Steven Woolf, Reta Madsen, and Maritia Woodruff, I learned not only how to act, but also how to write, direct, and produce. One of my teachers, Tony Kushner went on to win the Pulitzer Prize.

After school, I went back to Nashville and started a theatre company. My acting, directing, and writing got stronger. I met the love of my life, Betsy Sullenger and then, I headed to Los Angeles.

But life is strange. It always throws you a curve ball when you least expect it.

My first day in LA, I got a job delivering packages. I needed to make some money and this seemed like a good way to make it until I got an acting job.

The first house I went to (in Beverly Hills) I saw a little boy sitting on the steps memorizing lines. He was on his way to an audition, and he was having a really hard time getting the scene right. So I sat down and helped him. His mother came outside and before I could introduce myself the boy said, "Hey Mom, meet my new acting coach!" Well, I helped him for an hour. I helped him so long that I got fired from my package delivery job.

But the kid went to his audition and got the biggest TV job of his little life. The mother told the boy's agent about me. And the next day I had a bunch of clients.

That was eighteen years ago. Since then, I have coached over 6,000 kids and done workshops for another 25,000. In the mean time, I have continued my acting career. I've been in over 100 plays, 50 commercials, and I've starred in two television series, (for one of them, I got nominated for an Emmy). And my wife, Betsy, has gone on to become a movie producer.

And it all started because when I was little, I put on plays in my backyard. I've been very lucky. But I have also practiced a lot, too. I believe "private victories precede public ones." That means you have to succeed at home before you can go out and succeed in public.

And now with the Hollywood 101 series, you have a set of books that can help you.

Work smart,

Chambers Stevens

Helpful Hints for a Great Audition

Rule One: Learn what a monologue is.
This is a mistake I see over and over and over again. A monologue is ONE person talking. ONE person. Usually this one person is talking to either another person or maybe to the audience. A scene, on the other hand, is two people talking to each other. During an audition, a single actor should never perform a scene where they play both characters.

Rule Two: Research the kind of show your audition is for.
Are you auditioning for a comedy, a drama or maybe a musical? Many actors make the mistake of doing a big dramatic monologue when they are auditioning for a comedy. Or a Shakespeare mono- logue when they are auditioning for a musical. The rule is simple. Tailor your monologue to the kind of show you are auditioning for. Auditioning for comedy? Show you can be funny. Auditioning for a Shakespeare play? Do a classical piece.

Rule Three: Find out how long your monologue should be.
Usually the producers holding the audition tell you how long they are giving you. I have seen thirty-second monologues, one-minute monologues, and ninety-second monologues. With agents in Hollywood they usually don't care. Never go over two minutes unless someone specifically asks you to. Whatever amount of time they give you, make sure you do not go one second over that. A mistake I often see is an actor trying to do a forty-second mono- logue in thirty seconds. You know how they try to do this? They talk fast. Don't do this. It never works.

Rule Four: Pick a monologue that is right for you.
One of the biggest mistakes I see actors make during auditions is picking material that is not right for them. Believe it or not, I have

seen many sixteen-year-old girls do pieces about getting a divorce. And fourteen-year-old boys do pieces about raising kids. Pick a monologue that is within your age range.

Rule Five: Memorize your monologue.
Here are some keys to help you memorize.

    A. First read it out loud twenty times.

    B. Memorize the monologue word perfect.

    C. Test yourself to see if you have it memorized. Get out a deck of cards. Lay one of each suit (Hearts, Diamonds, Clubs, and Spades) face up on the table. Then say your monologue while you put the rest of the deck in the proper pile. (Hearts on Hearts, Diamonds on Diamonds, etc.) If you can do your monologue and divide the cards at the same time, you have your monologue memorized. If you can't, you need to work on it more.

Rule Six: Decide what the character in the monologue is trying to accomplish.
Is he trying to convince someone of something? Or is she trying to hurt someone? Then play that while you work on the monologue.

Rule Seven: Perform your monologue ten times before you show it to anyone.
Go to your bedroom and perform it ten times without messing up. If you mess up, start again. Performing it only for yourself will help you get it smooth. Make sure you are performing it out loud.

Rule Eight: Show it to at least five friends before you go to the audition.
This will help build your confidence.

Rule Nine: Go over your lines ten minutes before you do it.
This will warm you up for the audition.

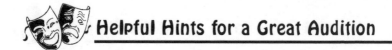 # Helpful Hints for a Great Audition

Rule Ten: Look either above or right at your audience.
This will help you connect with the people you are auditioning for.
Many actors perform their monologues in profile, or worse, by
looking at the floor.

Rule Eleven: Pause at the end of your monologue.
Take a couple of seconds before you walk away. This will give the
audition time to sink in.

Rule Twelve: Afterwards, go over your audition in the hall.
Did you do what you had prepared? Why not? Did anything throw
you? Did you do better than you had hoped? Why?

Rule Thirteen: Reward yourself.
I always reward myself after an audition. That way, no matter how I
did, I have something to look forward to. Your reward can be as
small as ice cream or going to a movie.

Here are some mistakes I see actors make. Don't make them.

Things never to do:
    1.   Use a gun in your audition scene. I don't care if it is fake.
Don't use a gun!

    2.   Give up. If you mess up in your monologue, plow through
to the end. We are all human. And humans sometimes mess up. I
have given call backs to actors who have messed up during their
auditions. Sometimes I will ask them to start again. But most of
the time, people who mess up just walk off. They give up. No
director wants to work with a quitter.

    3.   Use a funny accent. Unless the character you are audition-
ing for has an accent, use your own voice.

Helpful Hints for a Great Audition

4.   Practice in front of a mirror. This is a bad habit many young actors make. Mirrors encourage bad acting. Because you are thinking about how you look instead of what the character is trying to accomplish. So put the mirrors away.

5.   Do it like the character in the movie did it. This is a mistake that actors make when they pick monologues from a movie. No one cares if you can do a part exactly the way Johnny Depp did it. If you can't put your own personal spin on a monologue, don't do a piece from a film.

6.   Do an impression. Again, no one cares if you can do a Bart Simpson impression. There are very very very very very few parts where you do an impression for the whole show. Be yourself. Always the best advice.

7.   Wing it. 99.9% of the actors that try to wing it, bomb. Most of them bomb big. If you don't prepare, you will fail.

8.   Storm off if you mess up. Don't be a baby. No one wants to hire a baby.

30-Second Monologues for Boys

Garrett
(Big Trouble)

Okay I admit it. I lied.

I'm the one who used the last of the toilet paper.

I'm sorry, okay. Forgive me.

I know that I should have told Mom so she could have gotten some more.

But...I was embarrassed.

Because she knew we had two rolls left.

And she would have said, "No, we have two rolls left."

And I would have told her we didn't.

That I used them all.

And she would have asked why.

And it's disgusting talking about bodily functions with your mom.

So I didn't say anything. I'm sorry.

I didn't know there was going to be a massive snow storm so we're stuck in the house without toilet paper.

But hey, we're just going to have to buck up.

Now here, Grandpa has some extra diapers.

Everyone put one on.

Gage
(Mom's Revenge)

My mom's ambition in life is to embarrass me.
I'm not kidding. She told me that.
Yesterday, she came to school in a clown costume and
invited people to my birthday party.
Last week, she took my baby picture, you know the one
where I'm NAKED, and had T-shirts made and gave them
all to the cheerleaders.
And today, look at her, she dressed like a frog, and she's
dancing in front of the science lab to protest frog dissec-
tions.
(Yelling off) Okay, Mom, you win!
I'll make my bed.
I'll wash the dishes!
I'll even put the toilet seat down.
Anything, just please…GO HOME!!!

Ryan
(Shut Up)

(Ryan walks in and sees his parents in the middle of yet another fight.)

Everyone shut up!
I SAID SHUT UP!
Okay, that's better.
I can't believe you people.
You're supposed to be my parents.
Responsible.
Hard working.
Loving.
But all you ever do is fight.
And not even about important stuff, but you fight about stupid stuff.
Look, I'm tired of being in the middle of your arguments.
You want a divorce. Fine.
Get one. See if I care.
But don't expect me to live with either one of you. I'm going to my grandparents' house.

Steve
(I Need Water)

(Steve is working out with weights.)

999,997…999,998…999,999. One million.
(He falls flat on the floor. He yells to his family who is in the other room.)
Mom can you bring me some water…Mom? I'm dying in here…Mom, obviously you don't care about your son 'cause my throat is on fire! Dad, tell Mom I need some water…Dad! Dad! Your only son is expiring from thirst…Pam? Tell Mom to bring me some water. Pam, I know you are home. I can smell your perfume. Not that you smell bad. It's just…strong…Pam! Okay, Mom and Dad are going to be really mad with you because you let me die…Pam, Mom, Dad! Okay, I'm going to die now.
(He coughs.)
Bye everyone.
(He fakes a huge coughing dying fit. Finally he dies. A beat. Then he jumps up.)
Fine, I'll just get it myself.
(Steve exits.)

Michael
(Sour)

I love sour candy!!!

(He pops a sour gumball into his mouth.)

Wow!

Your tongue tingles.

Your mouth goes crazy.

And your lips…wow!!!!! They pucker up!

My mom hates when I eat sour candy because she says it makes me crazy. That is such a lie.

(He spazzes out into a strange dance.)

See, I'm normal.

Oh, and then when you bite down on the candy.

Zow!!!! Zuuuuuuuey!!!!! Zam!!!!!

It triples the flavor.

But my mom says it triples my weirdness.

That is such a lie.

(He spazzes out again.)

See, I'm normal.

I don't know what she is talking about.

I love sour so much, I wish they would make everything sour.

Sour pizza. Sour hamburgers. Sour toothpaste.

Sour bubble gum.

Wait, they already have sour bubble gum.

Yeah, that's what I need. Some sour bubble gum.

(As he spazzes off)

Zow!!!! Zuuuuuuuey!!!!! Zam!!!!!

30-Second

Monologues

for

Girls

Carly
(Super Talented)

When I grow up, I'm going to be the greatest actress in the world.
I'm already pretty good. Watch.
(She laughs really loud and then starts crying uncontrollably.)
Pretty good, huh?
I can also talk with a million accents.
(Carly plays two different characters having a conversation. Each line uses a new accent.)
"Hello."
"Hello."
"How are you?"
"I'm fine, how are you?"
"I'm fine, too. Nice weather we are having."
"It is a little hot for me."
Aren't I the best?
And I can also play guy parts, too.
(As a guy) "Baseball is cool. Football is cool. Girls are cool."
Wow, I'm so great.
I bet you thought for a while that I was a boy, didn't you.
Okay, so here's the scoop. I'm going to move to Hollywood next week. And I need some money for moving expenses. So how about investing in my career?
(In different accents)
"Please?"
"Pretty please?"
"Pretty, pretty please?"

Julieanne
(World Record Smiles)

Hello, is this the Guinness World Record's office?

Good, my name is Julieanne, and I've been smiling for the last seven days.

And I was wondering if that was a world record?

Wait, before you answer, I want to tell you that I even smile at night.

Look, here's a picture of me sleeping with a smile. Pretty good, huh?

I even smile when I'm sad.

Yesterday I found out that I didn't make the cheerleading squad and I was real upset.

I started to cry and smile at the same time.

Like this... *(She smiles and cries.)*

But I only cried for a minute because you know it's real hard to cry and smile at the same time.

So tell me please, is there a world record for smiling...there is?

(Jumping up and down) Yes! Yes! Yes!

How long is the record?

Two months. Two months?!?!?!

I have to hold this for two months?

(She starts crying again.)

Okay, I'll call you in two months!!!

More Kids' Monologues for Every Occasion!

Sheryl
(Deadly Drugs)

I don't understand people who take drugs.

First, they are expensive.

And it's not like you can go to the store and buy them.

Drug dealers are always selling them on the street.

And have you ever seen a drug dealer?

The ones in my neighborhood look like they could kill you. But if the police catch you, you go to jail.

And if they don't catch you and you take the drugs, you could die.

Die!!!

Imagine if pizza was like drugs.

I love pizza.

But if I could die from eating it, I think I would stick with spaghetti.

Maria
(Where's My Ear?)

Yesterday the most horrible thing happened.
My uncle came over to build me a tree house.
I designed the whole thing.
I even drew up plans.
So my uncle, Marty, brings his electric saw and lots of wood.
First, we measure each piece.
And then we put it on the ground and cut it.
Well, Uncle Marty told me to hold this one piece of wood in place.
And I'm holding it real tight.
Then the saw gets stuck in the lumber and Uncle Marty pulls on the wood real hard and the saw flies up and cuts his ear off.
It was horrible.
But Uncle Marty seemed really calm.
He just asked me to look around to find his ear.
Finally I found it in a pile of sawdust, but when I showed it to Uncle Marty he said that was the wrong ear.
His had a pencil stuck behind it.

Jasmine
(I Need A Bra!)

Every girl in my class has a bra, but me.
I've begged my dad for one but he says I don't need one.
Yes, I do.
I need a bra.
But he just laughs at me and says, "Honey, you are as flat as a board."
I asked him if I could at least get a training bra.
And then he asked me what I was training them to do.
Sometimes Dad's are so stupid.
Then the next week, my dad went on a business trip and when he came back, I stuffed my shirt with tennis balls.
He grabbed my arm and dragged me to the store.
Guess what he bought me?
Seven bras.
One for each day of the week.
The problem is they are way too big.
I need to buy more tennis balls.

Magnificent Comedic Monologues for Boys

Niles
(I Love Lunch Ladies)

Everyone I know is always complaining about school lunches.
How gross they are. How bad they taste.
Well, I totally disagree.
School lunches are the best food in the world.
Tasty. Nutritious.
And the women that cook the food?
Oh. I love them.
With their cute little hair nets.
And the way they always smile when they're slopping Chicken Surprise on your plate.
Where do they find such wonderful cooks?
They must steal them from the best restaurants in the world.
And where do they get their recipes?
At my school, they make a meatloaf that is to-die-for.
The crap my mother makes at home is terrible.
But at school, I just can't get enough.
And they always have such great salads, too.
My favorite is carrot raisin salad.
Who would have thought that a fruit and a vegetable could be so good together?
It's healthy.
The fruit keeps your bowels regular.
And the carrots help your eyes.
Wow, lunch ladies are so amazing.

Logan
(I'm The Best Player On The Team)

Coach, how come you didn't put me in to play today?

I'm ten times better than Herzog.

He double dribbles, and he can't shoot at all.

It was embarrassing.

And Collins?

I can make twice as many free throws as him.

You've seen me at practice.

Well, not this week 'cause I had to take my little brother to school.

But last week, you saw me make a bunch of free throws.

And Sorenson?

That guy is way too uncoordinated to play basketball. A couple of weeks ago when he and I went one-on-one…I beat him good.

Next time I come to practice, you'll see.

What?

When am I coming to practice next?

Well, I can't make it tomorrow 'cause I was going to take this girl to the movies.

And next week isn't good for me either.

I'm going to be mowing yards to earn enough money to go to Six Flags.

But some time in the future, I'll come to practice.

So how come you didn't put me in to play today?

Rico
(Give Me Back My Mom)

(Rico walks in.)

Hey Mom, have you seen my…?
Wow, look at you.
Is that a new dress?
You look great.
No, not great.
Amazing. Almost hot.
And you got a haircut, too, didn't you?
It makes you look five years younger.
And your fingernails are painted.
I've never seen you with painted nails.
And are those new shoes?
What's so funny?
Wait.
Smile again.
Your teeth.
You've had them bleached.
Let me see your arm.
Pull up your sleeve.
(He gasps)
You've had your Bugs Bunny tattoo removed.
What is going on here?
(He jumps back.)
I don't know who you are lady.
But what have you done with my mom?

Nick
(Loving Pooh)

It finally happened...I've hit puberty.

"I'm a man. I'm a man."

You know how I know I hit puberty?

Not because I have hair in various...places.

Please, I've been shaving my back since I was six.

No, I am a man because finally, after twelve long, frustrated years, I have finally got a date with Shanna Kelsey Morgenstern.

"I'm a man. I'm a man."

I've wanted to date that luscious hunk of female beauty ever since she punched me in the crotch in kindergarten. I still can't pee straight. And it was simple, too.

I just walked up to her and I said, *(looking up)* "Shannon will you go to the movies with me? I happen to have two tickets to Winnie the Pooh's Heffalump Movie."

And she was like, "Heck yeah. I love Pooh!"

"You do?"

"Please. I've always loved Pooh! I love to sleep with Pooh. Pooh is one of my favorite things in the world."

By this time everyone in the hall was staring at her.

But I didn't care, I wanted a date.

So I was like, "If you love Pooh, then I'm going to get you Pooh."

And she hugs me. Right there in the hall, and then she runs to homeroom singing, "I love Pooh. I love Pooh."

So that's how I became a man. All because of Pooh.

Andy
(Gorgeous Male Model)

(Andy struts on, in front of the mirror.)

Ladies and Gentlemen, the most gorgeous male model in the world: Andy Finkman.

(He makes the sound of applause.)

Thank you, thank you for your understanding and love. I know you love looking at me 'cause I'm so gorgeous and handsome. And it's true, it is not always easy being this beautiful. But when you are born hot, you have to strut your stuff.

(Andy struts like he's on the runway.) How was that?

(He makes the sound of applause.)

Now, I would like to show you some of my favorite male model poses.

This is my "I am so cool" pose.

(He poses.)

And this is my "I'm the most beautiful boy in the world" pose.

(He does the exact same pose.)

And this is my "every girl wants to kiss me" pose.

(He poses the exact same way again. Then he makes the sound of applause.)

Thank you. Thank you.

Well, that's all the posing I'm going to do today.

If you want an autograph, I'll be signing my book, Most Beautiful Boy In The World: Part One, at the back of the room.

(He poses.)

See you later.

And just remember, when you think of handsome, think of me.

Matt
(Loverboy)

(Matt runs up to Jenny.)

Jenny!
Hey Jenny, over here.
Can I talk to you a second?
Look, I've got something to tell you, but I'm kind of embarrassed, so I'm going to turn my back to you so I'll have enough courage to say it.
(He turns his back to her.)
Jenny, I like you.
A lot!
Tons!
In fact, I want to marry you.
And live with you for a hundred years.
And we'll have lots of kids.
Thirty or forty.
And someday we'll die together, and they can bury us side by side in a single casket.
So, what do you think?
(He turns around.)
Jenny?!?!?!
Where did she go?

Jake
(Dangerous Pets)

(Jake enters with a shoe box. Jake only has one arm.)

For my show-and-tell project, I have brought with me a dinosaur.
Go ahead and laugh, I know you think I'm making this up.
But just like the film Jurassic Park, I have collected the DNA
of a dinosaur from a fossil that I found on a rock behind the
monkey bars.
I took the DNA home. And with my auto celluarizer that I
made with a hair drier and my mother's toaster…I was able to
turn the DNA into a dinosaur.
And not just any dinosaur, but a Tyrannosaurus Rex.
The T-REX I have in this shoe box may be small, but it is highly
dangerous. For example, most of you have probably noticed that
I only have one arm.
Last night, when I was going to feed my TREX a cricket, it ate my
arm instead.
Only minutes ago was I able to stop the bleeding.
Now, how many of you would like to see my dinosaur?
I thought so.
(Jake puts the shoe box on the floor and removes the lid.)
Oh, there you are you little cutie.
(Jake puts his hand inside the box.)
Ow!!!! He tried to bite my finger off.
(Jake slams the top back on the box.)
I'm sorry; I can't let you see my little baby.
It's just too dangerous.

Freddie
(Monster)

(Freddie runs into his parents' bedroom.)

Mom! Dad! Wake up!

I just had this horrible dream that a monster was under my bed! It was terrible.

He had these long fangs, and his skin was green and hung off of him like a lizard.

And his breath was disgusting!

Every time he breathed on me, I wanted to vomit.

Oh, and he kept saying these weird things.

He had this scratchy voice, and he kept saying, "I've got your parents, and now I'm going to get you."

He started to move toward me, and I screamed and ran out of the room.

And then I guess I woke up and...Mom! Dad!

Wake up; you're not listening to me.

So I'm running down the hall. And he jumps for me.

And he's saying, "I've got your parents, and now I'm going to get you." So I ran in here. And slammed the door.

And then I woke up.

It was so real. It felt like it was totally real.

His breath. I can still smell it.

But I wonder what he meant by, "I've got your parents and now I'm going to get you."

Mom! Dad! Wake up!

(Freddie shakes his mom and dad.)

Ahhh! You're monsters. Run!!!!

C.J.
(Adult Language)

Yesterday, my mom and I were at the video store.
I asked her if we could rent this movie that I saw the ad
for on TV.
But she said, "No, it has adult language in it."
So I asked her about this other movie and she said, "No,
that one has adult language too."
So I pointed to another one and she said, "Nope, too
much adult language."
I asked her what exactly adult language is, and she said
she would tell me when I got to be an adult.
"That makes no sense," I said. "'Cause if I'm an adult and
I don't have a language, how will anyone know what I'm
saying?"
My mother told me to shut up, and then she made me
rent The Little Mermaid.
I told her The Little Mermaid was for girls, and she got
so mad and started saying all these words I didn't under-
stand.
Then this woman who works at the store walked over
and asked my mother to be quiet.
She said she didn't appreciate my mother using adult lan-
guage in her store.
So my mom grabbed my arm and we left.
Adults are so weird.

Zach
(Big Brother)

My big brother, Rocko, makes me sick.
He is great at every sport in the world.
He's quarterback on his high school football team.
On the off season, he's state champion in wrestling.
In the summer, he plays soccer.
And in the winter, he plays hockey.
Two weeks ago, he took a tennis lesson and this weekend he's playing his first tournament.
It's disgusting.
Guess what sport I'm good in?
Basketball? Nope. Can't shoot.
Baseball? Nope. Can't hit. Golf? Nope.
I can't even carry the bag around one hole without getting tired.
Give up? I'm good at nothing.
My brother says I just haven't found out what I'm good at. So until then, he made me water boy for all his sports.
It's hard. I have to run back and forth bringing everyone water.
At first, all the guys on the football team said I was too slow.
So I had to speed up.
They would yell, "Water!" And I'd have to run to get the water and then run over to the bench.
It's getting so they just yell "water" to watch me run.

(cont. next page)

Zach

(Big Brother cont.)

And I run, too.
So they can't say I'm slow.
You should see how fast I am.
I'm a lot faster than the guys on the team.
I'm so fast, I could probably run track.
That's it, track.
Track!
Why didn't I think of that before?
(He does a little dance and then sings.)
"I'm going to try out for track.
I'm going to try out for track."
Gotta go. I've got to practice.

Calvin
(Clown Wars)

My parents are fighting a lot.

I think they're going to get a divorce.

My mom keeps threatening that if Daddy doesn't stop cramming all his friends into the car, then she's going to leave him.

Then Daddy says, well, he'll leave Mom if she doesn't stop dying her hair bright green.

So to make him mad, Mommy dyed her hair bright orange.

Daddy got so angry, he went out and bought these huge shoes that were way, way too big for his feet.

He walked around the house yelling, (In a funny voice) "Look at my feet. Look at my feet."

So Mom bought this huge flower and sewed it on her jacket.

Then, she asked my dad if he wanted to smell the flower, and when he leaned in to smell it…she pushed a secret button, and the flower squirted water all over his face.

Dad jumped up and kicked Mommy in the booty with his big shoes.

Then Mom grabbed Dad's red nose and gave it a big honk.

(cont. next page)

Calvin
(Clown Wars cont.)

Dad then grabbed Mom's unicycle and threw it into the swimming pool.

Mommy was really mad then, so she grabbed him by the ear, took him outside, and shoved him into his little car.

Which was already packed with twenty-three of his friends.

My parents are so stupid.

They think they are being funny, but they are such clowns!!!

Comedic Monologues for Boys

Gabe
(Look Who Is Mayor Now)

Excuse me, Mayor Grant.

I'm Andrew Miller, and I want you to know you are going down.

See, I'm at City Hall to turn in my 5,000 signatures on a petition to declare my candidacy for Mayor.

Mayor Grant, you are going bye-bye.

And you can stop smiling.

'Cause I checked the law books, and there is nothing in there that says a kid can't be mayor.

What's wrong Mayor, you don't feel like smiling now?

Well, I've got to go; I've got a campaign to run.

And get your feet off my desk.
'Cause in a couple of months, it will be mine.

Tyler
(Space Wreck)

Dad, I have some bad news.

I wrecked the spaceship.

Wait, before you get mad, it wasn't my fault.

There was this comet that came out of nowhere and dented the left wing.

Our robot, CM9, was trying to fix it.

But the comet must have been radioactive 'cause when CM9 touched the wing, she exploded.

But don't worry, our other robot, MR8, started cleaning up the mess.

Well, most of it.

But it turns out, CM9 had an anti-tampering device, and when MR8 touched the heap of junk that used to be CM9, sparks shot out everywhere.

And now MR8 is spinning around in circles.

She was spinning so fast, that she smashed into your spaceship and busted the windshield.

So, I'm sorry about all the bad news.

But accidents happen. Oh, look, it's almost time for space ball practice.

Do you think I could borrow your space cycle?

Kevin
(A Roaring Great Audition)

Hey.

My name is Kevin, and I'm auditioning for the part of Simba in your wonderful play, The Lion King.

Now, since Simba is a lion, I have prepared a little monologue.

So here goes.

(Kevin does the next part as if he were a real lion.)

Roar. Roar. Roar. Roar. Roar. Roar. Roar. Thank you. Thank you.

How was that?

What?

The lion talks?

You mean like English?

What? He sings and dances, too?

What kind of crazy play is this?

Everyone knows lions can't sing and dance. Then next thing you'll be telling me is that all of the animals in the play sing and dance.

What? They do?

Uh…yes, I can sing and dance.

Give me a second to prepare.

(He stretches like a lion.)

Okay, here goes.

(He sings the lyrics to the tune of Row, Row, Your Boat. He also dances…badly.)

"Roar, roar, roar, roar, roar, roar, roar, roar, roar, roar."

Bret
(My Favorite Zits)

Look, I got my first zit.

Isn't that great?

Look, it's huge and red!

You know what that means?

I'm a teenager.

Okay, I'm not really a teenager.

But, if you look at my face you'd think I was a teenager.

My mom wants to take me to the dermatologist.

But I said, "No way. I like zits. I hope I get a whole face full. They make me look older."

Well, I've got to go rub some dirt on my face so my pores will get clogged with some more zits.

Got-a-go.

(As he exits.)

Mom, get away from me with that washcloth.

I'm not washing my face!

Magnificent Comedic Monologues for Girls

Sammi
(Gas)

Yesterday in class I bent over to pick up my pencil and I let one.

A big one.

Everyone in the class got quiet and looked right at me.

I said, "It was my chair."

And then I moved my chair around to try to make a fart noise.

But it just squealed.

I was so embarrassed.

And everyone was staring at me.

And I kept moving the chair around when finally, I couldn't stand it anymore and I jumped up and said, "Okay, I admit it, I farted!!! I am sorry. But everyone in this room has farted. If you eat food, you fart. In fact, the average person farts six times a day. And from now on when I have to fart, I'm not going to hold it back. I'm going to let it rip."

And I sat down.

I was waiting for everyone to start laughing at me.

When instead, they started to clap.

It turns out that a lot of people in my class felt the same way about their gas.

Soon, everyone in class was farting.

The teacher just has to make sure she opens the windows to keep the air clear.

Alysa

(Ear Piercing)

Dad, can I talk to you a second?
Have I ever told you how sweet you are? How lucky I am
to be your daughter? How lucky I…all right, all right.
For the record, I was not trying to butter you up.
Just hear me out.
I was at the mall, and I saw all these earrings I really
liked. 19 pairs in all.
Pearls, dangly ones, and my favorite, these big hoops.
But I can't make up my mind, which I like the most.
The pearls are classy, the dangly ones are fun, and the
giant hoops will really make everyone look at me.
What happens if I go to school and one guy likes me
because I'm classy and one guy because I'm fun?
How will I know which ones to wear? So, here's what I'm
gonna do. I'm the only girl in middle school who doesn't
have her ears pierced.
So, I want 19 holes in each ear.
That way, I can wear them all at once.
I know you don't want me to get my ears pierced, but if I
had 38 holes, ya know, 19 on each ear, everyone in
school will know who I am!
Dad, where are you going? Dad!
Can I at least get my belly button pierced?… my nose?
What am I supposed to do with 19 pairs of earrings?
Fine, fine!
I'll get a tattoo!

Eunice
(Singing)

Yesterday, I'm walking home from school, when this woman falls out of the sky and lands in a bush.
I run over to see if she's all right.
And besides a couple of scratches, she seems okay.
She's wearing this strange outfit and holding this wand-looking-thing in her hands.
So, she thanks me for helping her and tells me that she wants to grant me one wish.
So I tell her I want to be a singer, but I can't sing.
So she says, "Let me hear how bad you are."
So I sing, *(She sings horribly.)* "Row, row, row your boat."
"Stop," she says. "You're right, you can't sing."
And then she waves her wand and bam, I start to feel all tingly inside. And she says, "Sing."
And I go. *(This time she sings great. Like a pop singer with lots of vocal runs.)* "Row, row, row your boat."
I couldn't believe it. I give her a big hug, and she says thanks for helping her, and bam, she flies away.
Now I just need to find someone who can help me learn to dance.
(She walks off singing wonderfully and dancing badly.)

Millie
(Girls of America)

Girls of America!

Are you like me, a lover of dolls?

Barbies. Chatty Cathies. American girls.

Don't you just love dressing them up, giving them a hug, combing their hair?

Me, too! But what do you do when this happens?!

(She holds up a headless Barbie.)

Can you say little brothers? How could he do this?!

To my poor innocent doll.

I'm a good little sister. Do I smash up his Legos?

Okay, maybe I did once. Did I ruin his GI-Joes?

I can't help it if the lipstick didn't come off!

And it's not my fault if he didn't like it when I painted his tree house pink.

But to destroy my Barbie, to rip my Barbie's head off!

Girls of America, it's time we struck back!

It's time to chop up their Lincoln Logs, laser their Star Wars toys, and dismantle Bob the Builder!

Wait-a-minute, Bob the Builder is kind of cute. I have another idea!

I'll set him up with my Betsy Wetsy doll!

Betsy and Bob sitting in a tree.

What's that smell? It smells like pee! First comes love, then comes marriage, and look!

Bob built a baby carriage!

My brother's going to hate that!

Heather
(Haircut)

My life is ruined!
Look at my haircut.
I look like I went to a blind beautician, and she used a chainsaw.
I used to have beautiful, long, luscious curls.
I want my curls!
Give me my curls!
Hey, I heard vitamin E makes your hair grow.
What has vitamin E in it?
Eggs! Eggs must!
It starts with an E!
Or egg plant!
Or maybe chocolaty éclairs!
That's it.
I'll eat a dozen chocolaty éclairs tonight, and my hair will grow back.
Of course, I'll be fat from all the sugar.
I'm ruined!
I can't go to class tomorrow.
Tomorrow is the first day of school!
I can't go!
One look at this haircut and they'll put me in boys' gym.
This is the last time I let my little sister cut my hair.

Vanessa
(A Big Spanking)

(Vanessa and her friends come running into the chambers of the United Nations.)

Erica, Rosie, Carly, Leanna…lock the doors.
No one move!
My name is Vanessa and you, ladies and gentlemen of the United Nations are being held hostage.
We, the kids of the world, have united, and we have some demands.
Adults you've had your chance; now it's our turn.
First, no more wars.
You people are always fighting over the stupidest stuff.
Can't you get along?
Under our leadership, everyone will play together, and anyone who tries to start a war, will get a big "time out."
Second, food.
From now on, no one will go hungry.
Candy for everyone!!!
Third, no more staying up all night.
Adults, let's admit it.
When you don't get enough sleep, you get cranky.
Then you pick on us.
From now on, every adult has to go to bed by eight o'clock. We, on the other hand, can now stay up all night.
So listen, you better follow our rules or you're going to get a big spanking.

Marcy
(Lemonade)

Lemonade, lemonade!
Get your ice cold, fresh squeezed lemonade!
Only a thousand dollars a glass!
Please, I beg of you, buy some lemonade.
See, my mom is making me save up for my very own cell phone.
Texting is like, my favorite thing in the world, and I figure a thousand bucks should cover the first month's bill.
LOL.
Last week, I had a bake sale and sold a whopping fifteen pans of brownies!
The second I opened up my stand, a nice lady drove up and said she needed something homemade and delicious for a potluck.
She gave me a new, crisp one hundred dollar bill!
Just as she was pulling away, my dad ran out of the house holding a brownie in his hand and screamed, "Marcy! Do not sell those brownies! You put salt in them instead of sugar!"
But it was too late; the lady was gone.
Can you imagine that potluck?
I hope they had enough water.
So, I am now selling lemonade.
Oh, delicious!
(Tastes lemonade, makes a disgusted face, and spits it out.)
EEK! Oh no, I did it again!

Joy
(Field-Trip)

Mom, I need you to sign this permission slip for a field-trip. My class is going bungee jumping. This just says that you won't sue the school if my leg snaps off.

Don't worry, it's never happened before.

Though last year, Amber Capogrossi only put the rope around one leg and now it's a foot longer that the other. It makes her walk funny but hey, she always takes first in the potato sack race!

Oh, and you need to sign this form, too.

This gives the Coast Guard permission to pick me up in case the rope snaps and I land in the river. That happened last week to a sixth grader. Her mother didn't sign the form and last we heard, she floated out to the Mississippi. I hope they catch her before she reaches the ocean. I heard she's scared of dolphins.

Eee!

What do you mean, you're not going to sign it?!

But all the kids in school will think I chickened out.

Fine, be that way.

At least sign the back of my report card.

(The mom signs it, and then Joy pulls it back fast.)

Bye, thanks a lot! You just ruined my entire school year!

(The mother walks off.)

Yes!

She didn't see that I got a D in English.

Rory
(Diapers)

Dad!

I wet my bed!

I know, I know I'm too old to pee in my bed.

I couldn't help it!

I had a dream where I worked at a Cola factory and I was a taste tester.

I had to taste every bottle, and the conveyer belt kept going faster and faster and I had to drink faster and faster.

Next thing I knew, I woke up, and I had pee'd in the bed.

And the worst thing about it was that I really liked that job!

I got paid twenty dollars an hour!

That's more than I make babysitting.

And there was a really cute guy, who worked right next to me.

And he was flirting with me the whole time.

So, when I go to bed tonight, I'm going to go back to work.

So, when you go to the store later on, can you pick me up a case of diapers?

KaTerie
(Sleepover)

Psst, Becky, Becky! Are you awake?
Is it just me or is this the most boring sleepover in the world? My big sister says that you're supposed to play tricks on people at sleepovers... like put someone's bra in the freezer. But everyone's too young here to wear a bra. So what else can we do?

We could put one of their hands in cold water and one of their hands in hot water. Supposedly that makes them wet the bed. That won't work, if anybody pees on my mom's carpet, she's the one that's going to be pissed.

I got it! We could shave off everyone's eyebrows! My sister did that to me and I looked surprised for six months, like this! (makes surprised face) No, that won't work. Everyone will be mad at me and won't come to my house again.

I got it! We'll wake everyone up and tell them that we played a trick on them. Then they'll wonder what we did! And all day long we'll make them guess but they can't 'cause we didn't do anything. Yeah that's a great idea. Let's do it! Becky? Becky? She's asleep again.
My parties are sooooooo boring.

Angelica
(Art Project)

(Angelica is putting her school books in her back.)

See you later Mrs. Gage…What do you mean I forgot to turn in my art project. That was due today?
What if I don't have it?...An F!!!!!! *(She drops her books.)*
No. I can't get an F! My Mom will ground me for life and then when I die she'll ground me for eternity.
(Obviously lying) Now I must have my art project in here somewhere. *(She rips open her bookpack and starts rummaging through it.)* I worked really hard on it. It took me almost a week…I mean a month to finish it. Oh yeah, here it is. *(She pulls out a blank sheet of white paper and hands it to her teacher.)* Okay, I'll see you around Mrs. Gage. Don't forget to give me an A. *(She starts to walk out.)* What?...What do you mean that is only a blank sheet of paper. I am surprised at you Mrs. Gage. I would have though a great art teacher like yourself would be able to look at my project and see it for what it truly is. What is it? *(Getting nervous)* You mean you really can't tell?...I can't believe I'm going to have to explain it to you. Okay here goes. *(She takes the blank sheet of white paper back.)*
It's a white cow in a snow storm.

Kaitlin

(The Ultimate Babysitter)

Hello, Mrs. Stillman. I'm here to baby-sit.

Oh, hi, Mr. Stillman. Look how good you look in your tux. Oh, congratulations on your award. Salesman of the year is a big honor.

Where are the little ones? Watching TV? That's great. Well, I know you want to get going, so I'll just be a second. Okay, let's start with the price. As you know, I charge ten dollars an hour. I know that's more than minimum wage. But these are your children and nothing is too good for Jacob and Megan. Now let's talk about the add-ons. If you are a minute past eleven, then I start getting time-and-a-half. A minute past midnight, I make twenty dollars an hour. If the kids throw up, there is an extra twenty dollar disgusting charge. That also goes for dirty pants and anything hanging out of their noses.

If Jacob wants something to eat, there is a five dollar cooking fee. If the dish that Jacob wants has more than two ingredients, then it's five dollars extra per ingredient. Example, a peanut butter and jelly sandwich is ten dollars. He wants juice with that, it's fifteen. He wants me to cut off the crusts from his bread, it's two-fifty a cut. If he wants a pizza, then I charge two-fifty if I cut it in a pie shape and three dollars if I cut it square.

Now, TV. If the twins fight over the remote more than once, I have a two dollar annoyance fee.

(cont. next page)

Kaitlin
(The Ultimate Babysitter cont.)

And if they hit, pull hair, or spit at each other, I charge forty-five dollars to get in the middle and break it up. Look, I've outlined all my extra expenses on this bill. Now, have fun. Mr. Stillman hold still, let me straighten your tie. That's better. And look, it's only an eight dollar grooming fee. Goodbye and don't worry, your little brats are in good hands.

Brooke
(What's That Smell?)

Oh, what is that smell?

Oh, it's you.

What is that you're wearing?

You smell like someone broke a perfume bottle over your head. Is your nose broken? What's that?

I can't hear you 'cause your cologne is so loud.

I'm so embarrassed; everyone at school knows my brother wears way too much cologne.

You know, if you would shower, you wouldn't have to cover up your body odor so much.

Step back.

New ten feet rule.

Any closer and I'll zap you with water.

Man do you smell.

Though there is one good thing. If you get sprayed by a skunk no one will notice.

Winnie
(Love Your Brat)

I'm a brat. A big brat. Watch.
(She lies on the floor and throws a major tantrum.)
Pretty good, huh? I do it all the time. Whenever my
parents try to boss me around, "Lisa, clean your room."
(Jumps on the floor) No!!!
(Jumps back up) A couple of minutes of that and my
mother cleans my room for me. My dad is a little harder.
I have to make him feel sorry for me. Just last night he
said, "Lisa it's time for bed."
(She jumps on the floor.) No one loves me!!! You just
want me to go to bed 'cause you hate looking at me!!!
(She jumps up.) My dad got so upset, he let me stay up till
two in the morning. Of course today I missed the bus
and had to walk to school. And I got there late. And
they were having a birthday party for my teacher, Ms.
Horner. And 'cause I was late, there wasn't any cake left.
And I left Ms. Horner's present at home. And all the kids
laughed at me 'cause I didn't get her nothing. You know,
come to think about it, being a brat is not all that fun.
(She smiles at us.) No, I'm just kidding, I love it. *(She
jumps on the floor.)* I WANT CAKE! I WANT CAKE!

Lisa
(Sadie Hawkins)

Stop!!!

Jess Morgan, you move one muscle and I'll kick your butt. As you know, this is Sadie Hawkins day. Which means that I can ask you out. And you have to say, "Yes." So, Jess Morgan, will you go out with me? Don't say anything. I just want to enjoy this moment.

(She sings.)

"You have to date me. You have to date me...ha, ha, ha, ha, ha, ha." Man, I love Sadie Hawkins day. The one day that women rule the world. The rest of the time you stupid men get everything. Don't look at me like that, you know I'm right. But not today. Today we rule the world. Jess, I'll pick you up at 6pm. Be waiting. And don't forget to wear something cute. I'm taking you somewhere nice.

Erica
(Tooth Fairy)

Okay, get up. Mom, Dad, on your feet. Wake up! Now look at this. What do you see? Come on Mom, speak up. Right. It is a quarter. A quarter. Not a dollar. Not ten dollars. Not a hundred dollars. But a quarter. And where do you think I found this quarter? Dad, your turn. That's right, sleepy head. I found this quarter under my pillow. And do you know why? I'll tell you why. Because I lost a tooth. A tooth that has been in my mouth a couple of years. Yesterday it fell out. And like millions of kids around the world, I put my little tooth under my pillow. And what do you think I found this morning when I woke up? That's right, Mom. I FOUND A QUARTER. Look, I don't know if there is a tooth fairy or not. But I do know there is not a thing in the world that you can buy with a stupid quarter. Candy. Nope. Costs more than a quarter. Clothes? Toys? You can't buy diddly with a quarter. So look, this is how I see it. Grandma just got false teeth. She paid nine hundred dollars for them. Twenty teeth into nine hundred is forty-five dollars. So look people, either find the little tooth fairy or get your purse, 'cause someone owes me MONEY.

Hayley
(Pop Quizzes)

Mrs. Taylor?

Can I ask you a question about the pop quiz you gave last Thursday?

I understand teachers love pop quizzes because they really get to stick-it to the students.

But as you can see from the PowerPoint presentation that I have made, I aced the last ten pop quizzes you gave.

And frankly, Mrs. Taylor, these tests are getting a little boring.

Come on lady, give me a challenge!

You know, like translate the quiz in French.

Or better yet, blindfold me and type it out in Brail!

Oh, I don't know, make me do the quiz while I'm standing upside down having to type the answers using only my tongue.

Anything to challenge me!

Anything to make it a little harder!

The way I see it, I've got nine more years of school, and if I have to keep taking these baby tests, I'm going to go insane!

I wonder if Einstein started like this?

Lori
(Boy Crazy)

My big sister is sooooooo boy crazy. I don't get it. What is the big deal? Boys are disgusting! They eat with their mouths open, and they're always dirty. But my sister doesn't care. Every time she gets near a boy, she screams. Like this. *(She screams.)* And if she sees two boys, she screams like this. *(Screams twice.)* And then if there is a big group of boys, she does this. *(Screams and totally spazzes out.)* The boys always look at her like she is a total freak. Which she is. Sometimes she calls a guy on the phone just to hear his voice. And so he doesn't know it's her, she pretends to be a salesperson. Like, "Uh hello, this is the Pizza Factory, and we just wanted to know if you might like some Pizza today?" Then the guy is like, "Cheryl? Is that you?" and she goes, "Yeah. How did you know it was me?" And the guy says, "I have caller ID." My sister is sooo stupid. Boys are killing her brain cells.

Magnificent Dramatic Monologues for Boys

More Kids' Monologues for Every Occasion!
Copyright © 2009 by Chambers Stevens

Weston
(Deadly Lying)

The first time I saw my brother drink, I was eight.
He's older than me, and he never lets me forget it.
The first time, I saw him steal some wine from my parents' liquor cabinet. He drank a bunch.
And then poured grape Kool-Aid in the bottle so they wouldn't know.
He told me not to tell, and I didn't.
When I was nine, he got this guy up the street to buy him a six-pack of beer.
He offered me one but I said, "No."
He told me not to tell, and I didn't.
Last year, when my parents went up north to see my grandmother, my brother came home drunk.
His friends drove him home. He was too messed up to drive.
Dad called and asked if we were all right.
My brother told me not to tell Dad that he came home drunk.
And I didn't.
Well, last night my brother got drunk again.
But this time there wasn't anyone to drive him home.
So he drove home by himself.
He crashed the car into a telephone pole.
His neck is broken, and the doctors don't think he'll ever walk again.
I should have told someone my brother was drinking.
I was trying to be a good brother.
But it turns out I wasn't.

Kris
(Laid Off)

My dad lost his job.

Everybody at his plant lost it on the same day.

He said we might have to move.

But until then, we're not allowed to spend any money. I asked him how come the plant closed down.

And he said the stock market was in bad shape and people weren't buying that many new cars anymore, so they closed.

But how could that be?

People need cars.

Cars break down.

People need new cars.

If my dad's not making them, then how will people be able to buy them?

I told my dad this, but he says he doesn't have time to explain it.

He's got to find a new job, or we won't be able to eat. I walked away, but I turned around to say something and I saw my dad had tears in his eyes.

I'm scared my family and I are going to starve.

Franco
(Bullying The Bully)

Jeff, there you are!

I've been looking everywhere for you.

Wait, where are you going?

I want to talk.

I was at home watching Sponge Bob Square Pants when my little brother came home crying.

His clothes were dirty, and his jeans were ripped.

I asked him what was wrong, and he told me that you had pushed him down.

And then you kicked him.

I told my brother that was impossible 'cause Jeff is bigger than you.

But my little brother says you beat him up.

Is this true?

What, you don't want to answer?

Okay, that's fine with me.

But get this, if I see you even look at my little brother again, there is going to be trouble.

You got that?

Now run along, I'm missing Sponge Bob.

Magnificent Dramatic Monologues for Girls

Alexandra
(Stop Smoking)

Yes Judge, I would like to speak to the Court.
Ladies and gentlemen of the Jury.
There has been a lot of testimony in this trial.
You've heard a lot about what a little brat I am.
And how I'm so spoiled.
But this is the first time you've heard from me.
The fact is, this case is about one thing.
My parents smoke.
And I don't want them to smoke around me.
It's that simple.
Imagine my life.
I get up, I smell like smoke.
I got to school, and I smell like smoke.
I come home from school, and my mom is still smoking.
And guess what the first thing my dad does when he
walks in the door? Light up a cig'.
So, I go to bed smelling like smoke.
Cigarettes are taking years off my life.
And recently I've been diagnosed with asthma.
Which you heard Dr. Des testify is aggravated by
smoking. Look, I love my parents.
I know they think they love me.
But actions speak louder than words.
If you have a kid and you smoke around them, you are
damaging them.
That's the truth.

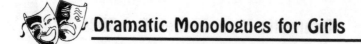

Ellie
(An Apology)

(On the phone)
Ashley, this is Ellie...don't hang up.
I wanted to apologize for how I acted today at school.
I don't usually talk about people behind their backs.
But today I...I don't know. I'm sorry I made up those stories about you.
I already called the girls at my lunch table and told them I was lying.
If it makes you happy, they are really mad at me.
Natalie said she was never going to talk to me again.
Anyway, I'm sorry that I lied.
Will you forgive me?
You will? Great.
You want to come over?
My mom just made brownies...okay see you in a couple of minutes.
And hey, thanks for being a real friend.

Lindsey
(Death)

Hey, Grandma can I talk to you a second?

If you want to be alone I understand…okay.

Look, I just wanted to say that I know you are sad about Grandpa dying.

You've been married to him over fifty years.

And I can't even imagine what that's like.

He was a great man.

Always smiling.

And remember that time I got stung by a bee and he rubbed whisky on my leg?

The pain went right away.

Grandma, I know I can't get rid of your pain.

You hurt too much.

But remember what Grandpa always said, "When you have a frown, turn it upside down."

So Grandma, how about giving me a smile…that's better.

Now let's go in the kitchen and make some peanut butter and banana sandwiches.

You know how much Grandpa liked those.

From now on whenever I eat them, I'll think of him.

Veronica
(Abuse)

I can't remember the first time my dad hit me.

He's been hitting me and my sister all of our lives.

I used to tell people I had all these bruises 'cause I fell down a lot.

Everyone believed me, too.

Except Miss Ray.

She knew something was wrong.

Then Dad got mad at me 'cause I left my bike out in the rain.

And he gave me a black eye.

Well, that's when Miss Ray decided to do something.

She called the school counselor.

I told them I had fallen down and hurt my eye.

But they didn't believe me.

I didn't want my dad to get in trouble.

But they said he didn't have the right to hurt me.

So I told them the truth.

The police came and arrested my dad.

And now he is getting some help dealing with his anger.

And my sister and I are safe for the first time in our lives.

Shari
(Cancer)

When the doctor told me I had cancer, I didn't even
know what that was.
He said I was very sick.
My mother started crying really hard.
She hugged me like I was going to die any second.
The doctor gave me lots of medications to take.
And I also had to come in to his office once a week to
have chemo. treatments.
All my hair fell out.
And I got really weak.
But I knew that I would survive.
'Cause every time I saw the doctor, he looked me in the
eye and said, "Shari, I know you feel terrible. But you're
going to make it. And you have to promise me on the
day that you finally beat the cancer, that you and I will go
to Disneyland."
Well, guess where I'm going today?
I can't wait to ride Space Mountain.

Glossary of Industry Terms

Show business has its own interesting vocabulary. The word *wings*, for example. When someone tells you to go *stand in the wings*, they mean stand on the *side of the stage*, not on the wings of a bird. I asked a number of the kids I coach to tell me their definitions for some of these important theater/film words. Sometimes kids can explain things more clearly than adults.

AD LIB - To make up words not already in the script. If a director tells you to ad lib, what he means is ignore the script and say something your character would say.

AGENT - A person who helps you get jobs. And then takes 10% of your earnings.

BEAT - A moment. If the script says, "A beat," then that means take a small pause before you say your next line.

BLOCKING - Stage Movement. When the director gives you blocking, he/she is telling you where to stand and when to move.

CENTER STAGE - Right in the middle of the stage.
(see diagram on page 73)

CROSS - When you move from one spot on the stage to another spot. This is like blocking.

CUE - Any signal that it is your turn to speak or move. If the director says "Pick up your cues," he/she means that when the other actor stops talking you must start more quickly.

Glossary of Industry Terms

CURTAIN CALL - At the end of the play, you come out and bow and wave to your parents.

DIALOGUE - The lines you speak from your script.

DIRECTOR - The person who is in charge of the play or film. He or she instructs the actors, set designers, and every other person/part of the play or film.

DOWNSTAGE - The front of the stage closest to the audience. The opposite of Upstage. (see diagram on page 73)

DRESS REHEARSAL - The last rehearsal before the play opens. The actors wear their costumes.

ENTRANCE - To walk on stage.

EXIT - To leave the stage.

FOCUS - Putting all your attention on one thing. If a director yells "focus," they mean "Listen up."

GESTURE - The way you move your arms and hands.

GREEN ROOM - The room where the actors hang out, waiting to go on stage.

HAND PROPS - Small items used by the actor. A purse or a baseball, for example.

HOUSE - The part of the theater where the audience sits.

Glossary of Industry Terms

IMPROVISATION - Acting without a script. Making it up as you go along.

LINES - The words you speak from the script. Learning your lines means to memorize the speeches your character has in the script.

MONOLOGUE - A character's long speech.

OFF BOOK - Being able to act without your script.

OFFSTAGE - The parts of the stage the audience can't see.

OPENING - The first performance of a play.

PROJECTION - To speak loud enough for the audience to hear you. If the director says *Project*, he/she means speak louder.

RUN-THROUGH - A nonstop rehearsal of a play.

SIDES - Part of a script. When you audition, they give you sides to read from.

SPOTLIGHT - A bright light.

STAGE LEFT - When you are standing center stage facing the audience, stage left is to your left. (see diagram on page 73)

STAGE RIGHT - When you are standing center stage facing the audience, stage right is to your right. (see diagram on page 73)

Glossary of Industry Terms

TOP - The beginning. When the director says, "Go from the top," he/she means start at the beginning.

UPSTAGE - The back of the stage. The opposite of Downstage. (see diagram below)

WINGS - The sides of a stage. If the actor stands in the wings, he/she is not seen. (see diagram below)

```
                    Backstage

        Upstage                    Upstage
         Right                      Left
                  Upstage Center

  W                                          W
  i                                          i
  n            Center Stage                  n
  g                                          g


              Downstage Center
       Downstage                  Downstage
         Right                      Left
```

Audience

x x x x x x x x x x

x x x x x x x x x x x x

x x x x x x x x x x x x

Bibliography: Magnificent Performances for TV By Young Actors

In my previous books, I've shared my favorite children's films and kids performances. But I am constantly getting email asking what TV shows I would recommend that kids watch. Here are my top 50. They are all available on DVD.

1. <u>The Partridge Family</u> – When I was a kid, this show about a family rock band that drives around in a colorful bus was one of my favorites. It's amazing how great it holds up. The songs still sound great. "C'mon, get happy!"

2. <u>The Brady Bunch</u> – "Here's the story..." If you don't know the rest of the opening theme song, you are missing one of the best family shows of all time.

3. <u>The Cosby Show</u> – One of our funniest comedians, Bill Cosby, in his first sitcom. Look for Raven-Symone in her first role.

4. <u>The Munsters</u> – Who knew monsters could be so funny? I've never met a kid who didn't want a pet dinosaur like Spot.

5. <u>Green Acres</u> – I recently watched a marathon of thirteen episodes of Green Acres. When I finished, my sides hurt from laughing so hard. Arnold is also the best pig actor in the history of television.

6. <u>Happy Days</u> – The best show about the 1950's. Film Director Ron Howard is great as Richie, but the real star of the show is Henry Winkler as The Fonz.

7. <u>My Favorite Martian</u> – What would you do if you met a Martian? And he moved in with you?

8. <u>Bewitched</u> – What would you do if you found out your wife was a witch?

9. <u>The Red Skelton Show</u> – Red Skelton is a comedian most kids today have never heard of, but at one time he had his own show that ran for twenty years! One of the funniest men ever!

10. <u>Good Times</u> – A very funny show about a poor family who lives in the projects. Esther Rolle is excellent as the mom who holds it all together.

11. <u>Mork and Mindy</u> – This is the show that made Robin Williams a star. Check out the later episodes when legendary funnyman Jonathan Winters joined the cast.

12. <u>Wonder Woman</u> – When my wife was a young girl, this was one of her favorite shows. Look for Debra Winger as Wonder Girl.

13. <u>The Monkees</u> – Silly, yes. But also a lot of fun. The Monkees is about a crazy rock group. This show helped launch the music video.

14. <u>Mickey Mouse Club</u> – The Club was created for the opening of Disneyland. Thanks in part to the catchy opening song, the show went on to be a huge hit. In the late eighties the show was remade as the All New Mickey Mouse Club. Britney Spears, Keri Russell, J.C. Chasez, and Christina Aguilera all got their start on The Club.

15. <u>Boy Meets World</u> – This winning series is even more successful now on cable. If you missed the first couple of seasons you can check them out on DVD.

16. <u>The Bernie Mac Show</u> – It's a blast watching Uncle Bernie try to raise three kids. He may be tough, but the kids have him wrapped around their fingers.

17. <u>The Amanda Show</u> – Amanda Bynes' show is Nick's version of The Carol Burnett show.

18. <u>Shelley Duvall's Faerie Tale Theatre</u> – Starring many famous actors and directed by Hollywood's hottest directors, Ms. Duvall takes the classic faerie tales and gives them a modern twist.

19. <u>The Abbott and Costello Show</u> – Slapstick from one of Hollywood's most famous comedy teams.

20. <u>That's So Raven</u> – Raven-Symone has the power to see into the future. Do you think she knew this show would be a hit?

21. <u>Martin & Lewis Colgate Comedy Hour</u> – The most popular comedy team of all time in their only television series.

22. <u>Make Room For Daddy</u> – One of the first situation comedies. Danny Thomas stars.

23. <u>Mr. Bean</u> –This is one of the most popular shows in the world. Rowan Atkinson plays Mr. Bean.

24. <u>The Waltons</u> – A touching family drama. Richard Thomas is fantastic as John Boy Walton, Jr.

25. <u>The Adventures of Pete and Pete</u> – Not very popular when it first aired on television. But now The Adventures of Pete and Pete is a cult hit.

26. <u>H.R. Pufnstuf</u> – A talking flute? A dragon in cowboy clothes? One of the strangest shows ever to appear on television.

27. <u>Doogie Howser, M.D.</u> – Life as a fourteen-year-old doctor.

28. <u>Sigmund and the Sea Monsters</u> – Here's what happened when a sea monster moves in with you. Another strange show from the Krofft brothers.

29. <u>Land of the Lost</u> – Teenagers caught in a time vortex where dinosaurs rule the world.

30. <u>The Incredible Hulk</u> – Based on the comic book, this series tells the story of when Dr. David Bruce Banner gets too much radiation. Next thing he knows, he's green and can pick up cars.

31. <u>Lost in Space</u> – A spaceship carrying The Robinson family crashes on a strange planet. "Danger, Will Robinson!"

32. <u>Lidsville</u> – A boy is stuck in a strange land where everyone is a hat? Charles Nelson Reilly steals the show as a magician named Hoodoo.

33. <u>The Worst Witch</u> – This British series based on the best selling books by Jill Murphy was an inspiration for the Harry Potter series.

34. <u>Clarissa Explains It All</u> – Before Melissa Joan Hart became Sabrina, The Teenage Witch, she starred in this Nick Show.

35. <u>Lassie</u> – Everyone wants a dog like Lassie.

36. <u>Eerie, Indiana</u> – A kid moves in to the strangest neighborhood in the world. Another wonderful show that was ahead of its time.

37. <u>Drake and Josh</u> – Nick's version of The Odd Couple.

38. <u>I Love Lucy</u> – Lucille Ball is the queen of comedy. If you haven't seen her in action check out her first series.

39. <u>What's Happening!!</u> – A comedy starring Fred Berry as "Rerun." Berry was one of the original break-dancers.

Bibliography: Magnificent Performances for TV By Young Actors

40. <u>Little House on the Prairie</u> – No electricity. No running water. No indoor toilets. That's life on the prairie.

41. <u>Laverne and Shirley</u> – Penny Marshall and Cindy Williams are hilarious in this spin off of Happy Days.

42. <u>7th Heaven</u> – The WB's longest running series.

43. <u>Lizzie McGuire</u> – The show that started it all for Hilary Duff.

44. <u>Fame</u> – This show inspired me to be an actor. It takes place at the High School of Performing Arts in New York City.

45. <u>The Little Rascals</u> – Sometimes referred to as the Our Gang series. Whatever you call it, Spanky and the gang are fantastic.

46. <u>Full House</u> – Here's where the Olsen twins started.

47. <u>Gilligan's Island</u> – By far the silliest show on the list. And one of the best theme songs in the history of television.

48. <u>Leave it to Beaver</u> – Yeah it's kind of corny. But it's still fun watching The Beaver get in and out of trouble.

49. <u>The Beverly Hillbillies</u> – One of the most popular sitcoms of all time. Granny, Jed, Elly May, and Jethro are all great characters.

50. <u>The Andy Griffith Show</u> – In my book there has never been a better TV series than The Andy Griffith Show. Ron Howard, who went on to be a huge film director, plays Opie.

Here are some good shows that are may soon be available on DVD. Keep checking the internet to see when they may become available:

<u>Amazing Stories</u>, <u>Batman</u>, <u>The Bionic Woman</u>, <u>The Carol Burnett Show</u>, <u>Christy</u>, <u>The Courtship of Eddie's Father</u>, <u>Dennis the Menace</u>, <u>The Donna Reed Show</u>, <u>Donny & Marie</u>, <u>Facts Of Life</u>, <u>Family Matters</u>, <u>The Famous Jett Jackson</u>, <u>Father Knows Best</u>, <u>Flipper</u>, <u>Gentle Ben</u>, <u>Head Of The Class</u>, <u>The Hughleys</u>, <u>Moesha</u>, <u>My Three Sons</u>, <u>The Patty Duke Show</u>, <u>Sabrina, The Teenage Witch</u>, <u>The Six Million Dollar Man</u>, <u>Small Wonder</u>, <u>The Torkelsons</u>, <u>The Wonder Years</u>, and <u>The Young Indiana Jones Chronicles</u>.

Index

Index

Monologues By Subject
Dramatic

Hollywood 101

The study guides for young actors serious about acting!

#1

Order Options: website **www.ChildrenActingBooks.com**

fax form below to 323-255-3616

call customer service 1-800-891-4204 M-F 9am-5pm PT

#2

Please send...

____ copies of Magnificent Monologues for Kids @ $13.95 ea. = ____
____ copies of Ultimate Commercials 4 kids/teens @ $14.95 ea. = ____
____ copies of Sensational Scenes for Teens @ $14.95 ea. = ____
____ copies of Magnificent Monologues for Teens @ $14.95 ea. = ____
____ copies of Sensational Scenes for Kids @ $14.95 ea. = ____
____ copies of Magnificent Monologues for Kids 2 @ $14.95 ea. = ____ #3

Shipping Charges	
1+ books	$3.95
2+ books	$5.55
4+ books	$8.45
7+ books	call

book subtotal = ____

shipping = ____

sales tax (CA residents only--add $1.23 tax for *each* book ordered) = ____

#4

Order Total = ____

Name: _____

Address: _____

City/State/Zip: _____ #5

Phone: (____) _____

Email: _____

Payment Method: ☐ Ck./MoneyOrd ☐ Visa ☐ MasterCrd ☐ Discover

Account #: _____ Exp. Date _____ #6

Signature (necessary)_____

"Chambers' expertise will take you on a road trip through Hollywood"
—*Barry Cohen*
Nickelodeon

Get the set and SAVE!
Kids Pack-n-Act Set
includes books #1,2,5
Teens Pack-n-Act Set
includes books #2,3,4

$39/set

Send payable to: **Sandcastle Publishing, P.O. Box 3070, South Pasadena, CA 91031-6070**